Edinburgh

Photographs by
Colin Baxter

Text by
Hamish Coghill

LOMOND BOOKS

EDINBURGH · SCOTLAND

Edinburgh

Edinburgh is a city for lovers. It is a city which grows on the visitor with every unveiling of its beauty and character – it is a love affair which can be kindled into a passion on the first sight of sunrise from a hotel window, or it can take time for the relationship to develop. Edinburgh can lay out all its many attractions in one glorious summer's day, or hide them away in nooks and crannies, enticing you to come and explore the old and the new, to grow in confidence as you tour the streets and rub shoulders with history at each turn.

'No situation could be more commanding for the lead city of a kingdom; none better chosen for noble prospects', said Edinburgh's son and author Robert Louis Stevenson. For this capital of Scotland (since 1452) lies between the Pentland Hills and the Firth of Forth, a situation which gives the new arrivals a startlingly different view from whichever point of the compass they approach: whether it is the first glimpse of Arthur's Seat, the distinctive old volcano stump which dominates the

EDINBURGH CASTLE AND PRINCES STREET GARDENS
Opposite: Winter bare, and the old fortress stands stark and proud above Princes Street Gardens. Above: Autumn in the gardens where once the Nor' Loch flowed as a natural defence to the Castle Rock.

CITY PANORAMA
Looking west from
North Bridge, towards
the Castle.

Royal Park of Holyrood; the skyline of domes and spires and steeples; the comforting strength of the ancient fortress that is Edinburgh Castle, which has protected its citizens through a riddled history of confrontation with the ancient foe of England or inter-party warring; or the changing character of a drive through the suburbs into the heart of a town divided into Old and New.

It was Stevenson who created Jekyll and Hyde, based on a notorious eighteenth-century town councillor, Deacon William Brodie. By day a respectable cabinetmaker, head of his guild, and decision-maker in the council chambers; by night, a rake and gambler, and eventually a house-breaker and thief who met his end on the gallows he had designed himself.

'Auld Reekie,' they call Edinburgh, or 'the Athens of the North.' Auld Reekie, the Old Town which clings tenaciously to the steep hill which links the Castle at one end of the Royal Mile to the Palace of Holyroodhouse where the Queen and her family base their regular stays in the city.

Although there are plenty of tours on offer, Edinburgh is a place to discover on foot. You cannot take a bus down the tight, steep closes off the High Street, you cannot nip into the fine hostelries and restaurants which adorn the ancient thoroughfare

RAMSAY GARDEN, (above & below opposite) Fairytale houses next to the Castle.

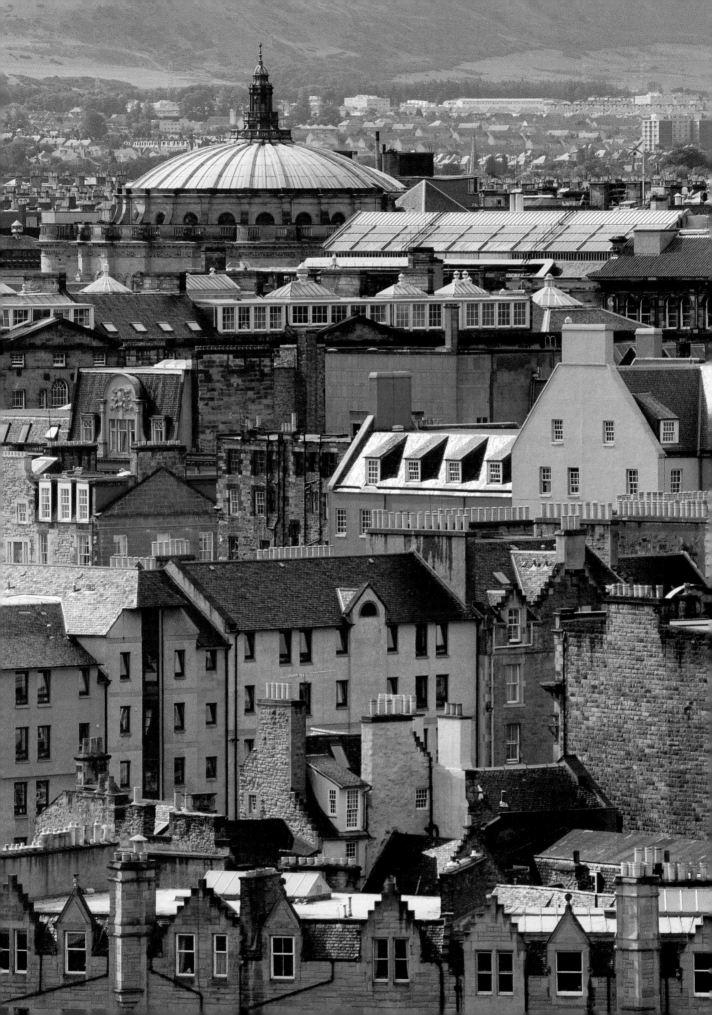

which has undergone a facelift – now pedestrian-friendly after a traffic-control scheme which has broadened the pavements and seen the roadway relaid with traditional granite setts (the cobbles of many Scottish cities).

The high point of the Royal Mile, literally, is the Castle. It has clung in some form to the rock for fifteen recorded centuries, and probably long before that. The first settlers in this part of ancient Britain found comfort and courage in its height over the marshy plains below. They looked out on a wilderness which ran to the sea on one side and across the old lochs and countryside to the protective band of the Pentland Hills on the other. They could see right down the coast, as you still can from the High Street today, across East Lothian to pick out the island of the Bass Rock, now a bird sanctuary off the coast.

It was natural, then, that the first wooden fortifications sprang up on Edinburgh's rock, and gradually a castle evolved as the town slowly formed with wooden and turf houses spreading down the slope.

The Castle has been besieged and withstood many assaults, it has been cravenly surrendered on occasions, but what has never diminished is its dominance of the city. It is the bastion on which the Old Town survived; it is the symbol of the city today. It is no coincidence that the two great fighters for Scottish nationhood stand one on either side of the entrance gate – William Wallace, the guerrilla leader, and King Robert the Bruce, whose victory on the field of Bannockburn against the English troops of Edward I brought an independence which the Scots fought hard over the years to retain – until they were sold down the river, many believe, by King James VI. He left his Scottish court with undue haste in 1603, to take up the throne of the united kingdom of England and Scotland, breaking his promise to return north at least once every three years.

WHITEHORSE CLOSE, Canongate. Crowstep gables, white walls and an elegant stone staircase. Opposite: Looking from Calton Hill, rooftops stretch across the Old Town to the domed McEwan Hall and Pentland Hills in the distance.

THE CITY AT DUSK

PRINCES STREET & SPIRES

A century later in 1707, Scottish nobles were bribed to enter the Treaty of Union, ending the Scottish Parliament and proclaiming London's control. It is a debate which still rages today, and one of the city's finest buildings, the old Royal High School in Regent Road, waits word of some form of Scottish devolution so it can again house an Assembly to manage Scotland's affairs.

The Castle houses the oldest building in Edinburgh, the chapel of St Margaret, queen of Malcolm Canmore (who put Macbeth from the throne in circumstances slightly different from those outlined in Shakespeare's play). The queen died days after the news of her husband's death in battle with the English, and her influence on the Scottish court, her prayerfulness and concern for others, brought her sainthood. The tiny chapel is simple, but full of reverence for a woman who brought light and goodness to dark days.

Nowadays, in summer, the sloping Castle Esplanade which leads up to the drawbridge doors is mostly a clutter of scaffolding as the seats for the renowned Military Tattoo are positioned. For three weeks there are spectacular military displays as the skirl of the pipes and beat of the drums ring

THE CITY FROM THE EAST
A view across the Canongate with the landmark clock tower of the Balmoral Hotel. Below: Princes Street, adorned with its many flagpoles, looking to Calton Hill beyond.

DEACON BRODIE'S TAVERN, Lawnmarket. It was Robert Louis Stevenson who created Jekyll and Hyde, based on a notorious eighteenth-century town councillor, Deacon William Brodie. The name of the character is remembered here in the Royal Mile.

out nightly over the town. The Castle floodlights are transformed by colour and by fireworks, and this carnival atmosphere spills over into Festival time.

It is then that the streets become alive, there is a special bustle and cheeriness which banishes the douceness which can afflict Edinburghers. The International Festival of Music and Arts runs for three weeks during August and September. While the renowned names pack audiences into the concert centre of the Usher Hall or the new Festival Theatre, in halls and rooms – none too small – the rising tide of young hopefuls clings to the Festival's skirts on the Fringe. More than 1,000 shows boost the official Festival programme, and when you add a Jazz Festival and a Film Festival in those crammed weeks, the visitor has to choose whether to pack in as many shows as possible, or take time off to explore; the energetic tackle both.

The Royal Mile and the open square at the Mound are the places where the Fringe performers test out their material, hoping to entice an audience on the strength of street performance. Off the High Street, closes ring to the sound of music and youthful declamation, and there is a buzz about

SHOP MURAL, corner of Broughton Place & Broughton Street.

the place which sweeps up most visitors.

Visitors also find their way into these closes, and here you are stepping in the footsteps of many of the great men of the city who were happy to live in the crowded tenements, ten, eleven, twelve-storeys high, long before anyone had thought of the term skyscraper. The sharp drop of the land from the spine of the Royal Mile to the north and south meant that tight, crowded town buildings had to be thrown high, and people had to be content to share land or tenements. Lords and ladies, judges and merchants, climbed the same stairs as the craftsmen and journeymen, albeit to homes on different levels. But they all had to step sharply when the infamous warning of 'Gardyloo' went out as a chamber pot was emptied out of a top window onto a reeking close below. 'Haud yer haun', was sometimes enough to escape a drenching.

JAMES' COURT, Royal Mile.

From the narrow entrance of many closes, as you traverse the Royal Mile – it is four streets in one, Castlehill, Lawnmarket, High Street and Canongate, – there are splendid views of the spreading city. Framed in the old stone archways, they make lovely pictures, and show where the Old Town proper ends and the sprawl, which was inevitable as the city grew in importance, begins.

The Canongate itself was once a small, independent town outside the city walls, and up its narrow main street came many a man and woman to face the ultimate penalty at the Cross of Edinburgh, a place of execution in times of great barbarity and cruelty. Those accused of witchcraft were reserved for the Castlehill, to meet a fate by fire, or alternatively by water in the old Nor' Loch beneath the Castle Rock. Ornamental gardens mask the graves of those flung into the murky waters – the prosecutors had a simple principle, if a condemned woman came to the surface she was definitely a witch, if she did not, she was innocent after all.

THE OLD TOWN
Opposite: The crown spire of the High Kirk of St Giles in the High Street has dominated the Old Town since 1500.

During State and other visits, the Queen, in either open carriage or swish limousine, travels the length of the High Street, often to the High Kirk of St Giles. Its crown spire is instantly recognisable on the skyline, and it is the centre of much of Scotland's history. It was here that the Protestant Reformer John Knox was minister, and his animosity was directed towards the Catholic Mary Queen of Scots; the tragic young sovereign who never mastered from her French upbringing the intricacies of Scottish intrigue, and who eventually fell into the even more complicated web of politics woven by her cousin Queen Elizabeth I of England, who ordered her execution. But Mary had the last laugh – it was her son James VI who inherited the British throne.

Much of Mary's time was spent in the Palace of Holyroodhouse, close by the Abbey founded by her ancestor David I. He had it built for his

THE CANONGATE TOLBOOTH

The Canongate Tolbooth is now a museum, but it housed a council and a jail when it was at the heart of the old burgh's affairs.

Augustinian monks in gratitude for his life being spared by divine intervention, as he hunted in the grounds surrounding the present palace. It is said he fell from his horse and a stag was about to impale him when a cross, or 'rude', appeared between its antlers and the animal was scared off. It was a Holy Rude, he believed, and thus he named his abbey in 1128. It was sacked by English troops in 1544 and although King Charles I had his coronation there in 1633 it gradually fell into disrepair. King David's monks, incidentally, left the city a great gift – they discovered that the wells and springs around Holyrood were perfect for the brewing of ale, and over the centuries the names of Edinburgh beers became renowned. Edinburgh breweries are still winning awards for their expertise.

The Palace has been open to the public for many years and much of its current appearance is due to the efforts of King Charles II who, on the Restoration of the Monarchy after the Civil Wars, had a new wing put

onto James IV's first tower and oversaw its extension. It is well-used by
Royalty, frequently on a 'bed and breakfast' basis when one or other of the
family slip into town to carry out an official engagement. The grounds of
Holyrood play host to the royal garden parties.

*CHARLOTTE
SQUARE,
A Robert Adam
masterpiece.*

MELVILLE STREET

The Old Town has undergone a tremendous renovation programme.
Places like the Canongate and the Cowgate had notorious slums in the
last century, families crowded into rooms in
conditions which bred rampant and fatal disease
amidst the poverty of the downtrodden. But a
sensitive and continuing programme has brought life
back into the oldest parts of Edinburgh, and it is a
living heart which beats strongly, backed by
organisations sympathetic to its needs and supported
by the cash that makes transformation and
improvement possible. In the upgrading, there has
been time to rediscover a touch of the past in the
recreation of an old Canongate garden in Dunbar's
Close, reminiscent of earlier days when less-crowded
pressures meant there was space for greenery and
shrubs, and now it is an oasis of beauty and stillness
off a busy thoroughfare.

After the scares of the Jacobite Rising of 1745 which
saw the Young Pretender, Charles Edward Stuart (as
romantic and tragic a figure as Mary before him) fill

*NORTH BRIDGE
AT NIGHT*

GREYFRIARS BOBBY,
George IV Bridge.
A tribute to the faithful
Skye terrier who guarded
his master's grave in
Greyfriars Kirkyard.

the town with his Highlanders before setting off for humiliation in England, and the final ignominy on the field of Culloden one murky winter's day the following year, the sheer pressure of people meant that the need for Edinburgh to expand was finally recognised.

There is a tombstone in the Canongate Kirkyard to the man whose vision made it possible, George Drummond, six times Lord Provost, and the driving force behind the idea of a New Town. He was an old man and died before he saw his dream turn to reality, and it was a young man, James Craig, only in his twenties, who produced the improvement plan which won the Town Council's prize of a gold medal and purse of guineas in 1766, and which with amendments was formally adapted in 1767. It is that strikingly simple concept of a grid which gives us the first New Town today; Princes Street, George Street and Queen Street, balanced at either end by the Charlotte and St Andrew Squares. The development of the New Town, the birth of Classical Edinburgh, the concept of Athens of the North, as stage followed stage through the eighteenth and nineteenth centuries, took the city into a fresh phase of its international reputation.

Although it clutched desperately to the slopes off the High Street, the Old Town was a centre of not only Royal court and Parliament, but a 'nest of lawyers', the centre of medicine and science, individual and challenging thought; it was a place where men like David Hume, the philosopher, and

Adam Smith, the economist, strolled the High Street; where Robert Burns found love and comfort and appreciation, where men of genius gathered to argue and discuss and plan boldly in a university town. This was the Golden Age, the end of the eighteenth century when the first New Town was taking shape and Edinburgh was at the peak of its intellectual prowess. Something which is happening again with a flush of new building to equal anything in Britain.

But it is to the New Town that prime architectural attention is paid; to the long straight streets, the carefully planned townhouses; it is realised in planning quarters that they cannot be swept away to repeat mistakes of the past. Many of the original four or five-storey houses are now offices, others are turned into apartments, with the servants' quarters in the basement now graced with the title 'garden flat,' and happily occupied by people who want to live close to the heart of the city and not be tempted to suburbia in Morningside, Blackhall or Corstorphine. It is a living city centre.

The New Town has been under threat, and almost daily there is a skirmish between the conservation and preservation bodies, headed by the

RAMSAY GARDEN IN WINTER
Eminent town planner Sir Patrick Geddes encouraged the development of Ramsay Garden houses to attract University dons back to living in the Old Town at the end of last century.

*THE PALACE OF
HOLYROODHOUSE
Edinburgh's royal
residence sits majestically
beside the ruined Abbey,
founded in 1128, in
Holyrood Park.*

Cockburn Association (named after the judge Lord Cockburn who wrote so scathingly on the efforts to despoil the city last century), and would-be developers. The New Town is deceptive in that it is not all spacious streets and graceful ornamental gardens. Again it is worth the visitor's time to step off the main roads and into the little lanes and meuses which proliferate. There are hidden charms waiting to be discovered, there are galleries tucked away in secondary streets, originally built for the working classes, one level down from the better residential streets.

The New Town was at first unpopular with the citizenry, and the town council had to offer inducements to persuade people to consider moving across the valley from their comfortable quarters with its hordes of taverns and clubs, with its street markets and jostling throngs, its mixture of all classes on the streets, even though the roadways were often cluttered with litter and the smells could be appalling. But once the move to bigger and airier houses, and a more comfortable way of life, and the stone townhouses with ample room for the many servants needed to keep a family in style were accepted, the whole atmosphere of Edinburgh changed. It became the custom to entertain in the dining room and

NORTH-WEST TOWER, THE PALACE OF HOLYROODHOUSE

VICTORIA STREET, runs from George IV Bridge down to the Grassmarket, and is packed with shops and restaurants of great individuality.

drawing room rather than to meet friends in the smoky, noisy convivial howfs or taverns off the High Street or in the Cowgate and Grassmarket. Carriages replaced the sedan chairs and the stout Highlanders who had earned a living carrying folk around were out of a job; shops and markets were needed to supply a new and growing population, and once the jump was made to the north, so the South Side also developed on the open countryside which surrounded individual estates and mansion houses around the town.

The nineteenth century saw the building of such gracious crescents as Moray Place and Ainslie Place, and streets further north. More building ground was opened up when Thomas Telford completed the Dean Bridge, soaring above the old Water of Leith Village which had nestled in the deep valley below for centuries, supplying the town with its flour for bread, and housing the headquarters of the baxters (or bakers). It still remains a village in the heart of the city, now called the Dean, and is built on both banks of the river which supplied the energy along its eighteen odd miles for the range of mills which helped to bring the city its prosperity.

From his snuff mill at Spylaw close to another village, Colinton (or Hailes), the eminent James Gillespie made his fortune, and like other prosperous men in the city before and after, bequeathed it to found a hospital school for orphan children. It was George Heriot, the Jinglin' Geordie treasurer to the often penniless King James VI and I who set the pattern, and wanted his Heriot's Hospital to look after fatherless bairns. The benefactors continued with George Watson, treasurer of the Bank of Scotland; Exchequer official Daniel Stewart; businessman Sir William Fettes; newspaper proprietor James Donaldson; John Watson and Mary Erskine, who all wanted to see the city share their good fortune. Today the old hospitals are mostly fee-paying schools, John Watson's houses the Gallery of Modern Art, and Donaldson's is a centre for teaching deaf youngsters.

Buildings like Heriot's School, Fettes College, Daniel Stewart's and Melville College and Donaldson's, reflect the wide range of architecture outside the New Town which helps to give the city its renown. There is also an exciting range of modern buildings, including the dramatic glass-fronted Festival Theatre in Nicolson Street and the distinctive circular

TOWARDS CALTON HILL, from the Castle Esplanade.

The chimney pots of the Old Town houses may not reek smoke these days, but are typical of their time. Across and above the valley is Calton Hill with, among its various buildings, the upturned telescope of the Nelson Monument.

International Conference Centre complex off Lothian Road.

There was a time in the 1950s and 1960s when a Georgian building or Victorian tenement which had fallen into disrepair or become an overcrowded slum, would simply be demolished and a building of the time put in its place. Thankfully, a halt was called to that type of regeneration, and now many of the older streets have been sympathetically treated by upgrading and stone-cleaning to enhance their outside appearance.

Nowhere has this been more apparent than in Leith, the Capital's ancient port, which still proudly considers itself independent of the city. After long centuries of control from the High Street, it finally earned its independence last century, only to be forcibly remerged with Edinburgh in the 1920s. The port suffered as the demands on its extensive docks fell, but now business is more diversified, although shipbuilding itself has gone. The modern Leith is a far cry from the days when sailing ships brought claret, Madeira wine, and all manners of exotic foods and other goods from Europe and further parts.

There are many parts of Edinburgh which, like Leith, still retain a distinctive character – the villages which were once in the open land around the town, and which have been swallowed up progressively. Many of these are very old communities based, like Corstorphine or Colinton, round an old church. In Colinton, for instance, you can see a mort safe which was used to protect fresh graves from the grave robbers, just as at St Cuthbert's at the West End there is a watch tower overlooking the yard.

There are villages like Cramond, which the Romans knew, nestling on Edinburgh's other main river the Almond, with tiny cottages spilling down to the shore; while up in the Pentland Hills are the lovely thatched-roof cottages in the hamlet of Swanston, a place familiar to the young Robert

THE SCOTT MONUMENT AT DUSK

PRINCES STREET
Opposite: Looking from Calton Hill along Edinburgh's famous thoroughfare. In the distance are the three spires of St. Mary's Cathedral in Palmerston Place.

THE CITY FROM SALISBURY CRAGS
The Castle dominates the skyline. Its commanding position on the top of Castle Rock has been the site of dwellings dating back to the Bronze Age.

Louis Stevenson as his family holidayed nearby. Downstream on the Water of Leith is Stockbridge. Now a bustling shopping and residential area, it was once a hive of mills and markets, and also home to two of Edinburgh's most distinguished artists, Sir Henry Raeburn and David Roberts. Another charming and distinctive old village is Duddingston with its own loch and nature reserve on the edge of Holyrood Park.

In the field of art, Edinburgh has the National Galleries of Scotland centred on the Mound, and the neighbouring Royal Scottish Academy, both housed in multi-columned buildings which grace Princes Street, still the main shopping thoroughfare for the city centre. Nearby in Market Street is the City Art Centre, an imposing conversion of an old warehouse into a magnificent municipal gallery, positioned opposite the Fruitmarket Gallery. The Gallery of Modern Art at Belford and occasional exhibitions in Inverleith House, in the centre of one of the finest attractions the city can offer a visitor, the Royal Botanic Garden, all help to attract the genuine art lover, while for museum buffs there is plenty to ponder.

The Royal Museum of Scotland is in a Victorian palace in Chambers Street, and the Museum of Childhood, situated in the High Street is as

much a place for children as a walk down memory lane for their parents. Edinburgh is rich too in its libraries, with the National Library of Scotland based on George IV Bridge, a repository for the nation's literary and written archives, facing the extensive Central Public Library, another munificence from a benefactor, this time Andrew Carnegie, the Fife lad who made his fortune in the steel business in America.

THE FORTH BRIDGE
One of the world's engineering feats.

GEORGE HERIOT'S SCHOOL

The distinctive dome of the Old Quad of Edinburgh University dominates the South Side, its golden statue glinting in the sun, and within is the magnificent Playfair Upper Library, one of the great rooms of the Georgian period. The university is now housed in many buildings in an expansion which, regrettably, saw the destruction of most of the charming George Square. The remaining row of houses on the east side looking onto the central garden gives a flavour of what might have been, had the square been retained. Literally thousands of students have gone out to spread Edinburgh's reputation as a city of learning. From the medical school, linked particularly to the Royal Infirmary, founded as far back as 1729, medicine has been offered to the world, and qualifications offered by the Royal College of Surgeons and the Royal College of Physicians are still highly prized, as many overseas medical men and women will testify.

NORTH BRIDGE
AND THE
BALMORAL HOTEL
To encourage Old Town
residents to move to the
New Town, the first
North Bridge was built.
The present arched
structure dates from
1898, and the Balmoral
Hotel behind was com-
pleted in 1902. It was to
the gracious living in
elegant houses like those
in India Street (opposite),
that professional people
were attracted.

Other leading Scots are recalled in the city's other universities. Heriot-Watt University is named after James Watt, the inventor of steam power, and Napier University honours John Napier, the Edinburgh man who developed logarithm tables. After many years in the centre of town, Heriot-Watt has now moved to a greenfield campus on the outskirts at Riccarton.

Some of Edinburgh's most glorious buildings reflect the affluence of the city in its banking and commerce halls. The Bank of Scotland headquarters dominates the Mound, the original link between the Old and New Towns formed by the earth dug out to prepare the foundations for the New Town.

Finance and insurance govern the operations behind the magnificent facades in Charlotte Square and less well-preserved St Andrew Square. The north side of the former square is universally recognised as one of the great architectural gems of Europe, a monument to the skill of Robert Adam, and a fitting setting for both the headquarters of the National Trust for Scotland and the official residence of the Secretary of State for Scotland.

INDIA STREET

ST GILES' AND THE TRON KIRK

After business comes leisure and as twice the host city to the Commonwealth Games, Edinburgh has taken enormous strides to meet the demands of participants in many sports. The Meadowbank Stadium has an international-standard track and games halls which are filled from dawn to dusk. The colossal new rugby stadium at Murrayfield houses Scotland's home games, and bowling greens abound. But look at a map of Edinburgh and it is the golf courses which dominate, helping to keep the greenery in the city. There are six municipal courses alone and many private courses within the boundary, not to mention the lure of East Lothian and places like Muirfield, a regular on the Open Championship circuit. At certain times you will even see bowmen dressed in green shoot arrows at targets in the Meadows. They are members of the Royal Company of Archers, the Queen's Bodyguard in Scotland, at practice.

Leisure includes shopping too. And for the visitor there is a very wide range of top-class specialist shops, as well as the attraction of Princes Street and shopping centres like the Waverley Market, close by the railway station, or the St James Centre, a handy place to shop, but most citizens will apologise for the planning bloomer of the 1960s which

ARTHUR'S SEAT
The sleeping lion shape of Edinburgh's own mountain, taken from another fine park: The Meadows.

29

PRINCES STREET
Looking from the top of
the Scott Monument, to
the west.

THE EDINBURGH
MILITARY TATTOO
This exciting show
entertains thousands
nightly at the Castle
Esplanade in August.
It is just one of a host
of events during the city's
famous International
Festival, which attracts
visitors from around
the world.

allowed it to be built in place of stone tenements on the old square there.

This city, possibly more than any other, is a city of shades, each shift in the weather brings out the warmth of the old stones, the glisten of the cobbles, the richness of a flower tub outside a gracious door. The spectacular clarity of light of an autumn dawn, or the glories of a summer's sunset reject Stevenson's warning: 'The weather is raw and boisterous in winter, shifty and ungenial in summer, and a downright meteorological purgatory in the spring. The delicate die early…'

'West Endy, East Windy', the townsfolk joke as they head for the welcoming warmth of one of the many hostelries, in places like Rose Street where the poet Hugh MacDiarmid wrestled words and thoughts with his fellow makars (wordsmiths), like city-born Norman MacCaig.

Edinburgh is a city of many contrasting beauties, both old and new. But it is Stevenson's Jekyll and Hyde city still, behind the exteriors there is always something worth having a look at more closely. It is a city to explore beyond its face values, to take time for the backwaters and to find the unexpected.

THE CITY FROM CALTON HILL

CITY SILHOUETTE